Digital Strategy

The Art of Digital Brand Design

By

Champion Muthle

ISBN: 9798473910506

DEDICATION

To my fellow Planners and Strategists.
Be brave, be bold, be true.
May the force be with you.

CONTENTS

ACKNOWLEDGMENTS

A special thanks to the Creativity Gods for this fun little primer.

1

Introduction

They say there are only two ways to grow a business: Product Innovation and Digital Transformation. The latter is now an $11 trillion industry and the focus of this book. Digital Transformation is a world in which hypertext and hashtags rule, and in which patterns, trends, and culture drive performance. Perhaps you're a newly minted Community Manager, Content Creator, or Digital Strategist. Perhaps you've been through a Collegiate Communications Program, some PR courses, and an internship or two. Now you've landed in the field and have a cursory knowledge of what to do. Your new job starts on Monday and you'd like to feel confident about what comes next; or perhaps you've been working in the field for a while already and would like to master your craft. If so this is the book for you.

Digital Strategy is a rather new field, one that continues to develop both inside and outside of advertising agencies, marketing firms, and brands. When I first started as a Digital Strategist at McCan in 2012, there were no books on Digital Strategy or lesson plans to guide you through. Social Networks like Facebook and Twitter had only just started to reach the world of business and brands. There was no one, other than a small handful of experts and bloggers, writing about Digital Brand Design. I had just come from the World Bank, where I helped lead Digital Strategy for the 2011 World Development Report on Conflict and Development. I was now Social Strategy Lead for McCann Worldgroup, reporting directly to Mary Perhach, our Chief Communications Officer. I was tasked with bringing order to the somewhat chaotic and informal network of social media channels being utilized by McCann and her sister agencies at the time, which included developing global privacy policies, guidelines, and frameworks for the future. It was a complex but rewarding challenge, one made all the more enjoyable by the talented and perceptive Mrs. Perhach, now the Founder and Owner of Swellshark in New York. At the time, I had only my experience and a few templates to guide me. I started with a competitive analysis of McCann and other global Ad Agencies, which tracked and measured their performance across a number of key indicators. The insights gained from this analysis helped catapult McCann into first place, firmly establishing the network as a leader in all things Digital and Social. My next task was to apply this thinking to McCann's impressive roster of clients and global brands, which at the time included: American Airlines, Burger King, Verizon, Mastercard, General Mills, Staples, the Army Ikea, Coca-Cola, and the McCann brand itself. My official title was now Digital Strategist with the remit to work across our entire portfolio of clients and serve as somewhat of an internal consultant to Creative Teams, Account and New Business leaders, and Executives.

Our new unit was called McCann Always On, one of the first micro-agencies (or Agencies within an Agency) dedicated directly to Digital and Social, which were, at the time, somewhat indistinguishable and interchangeable terms. Social Media Channels like Facebook and Youtube were still highly misunderstood in the context of brands and clients. Our job was to lead a new Digital Strategy Practice, which meant helping McCann's traditional clients transform into authentic Digital Brands and Businesses. The work was difficult and imprecise but highly enlightening. Again, there were no books like this one to help guide our path. In many ways we were implementing a whole new field of practice; everything we produced had to be original and standardized. Every template, deck, and tool had to be designed, developed and distributed ourselves, organically. It was great practice. I tried to bring the same spirit of social impact and cause to our team as I had in my prior roles. Facebook Causes made this a bit easier, but connecting the dots between brands and double-bottom lines was still a bit far off. That was until later that year, when our team inspired a social movement that pushed the bounds of Public Relations, Digital Strategy, and Social Impact. Our unit was now firmly established, and the role of Digital Strategy in the world of big brands and big business was now well established, too.

2

Digital Strategy 101

As Stormzy says, "first things first." What do we mean by Digital Strategy? How does it differ from traditional Strategy? What about Social and Integrated Strategy? Understanding Digital Strategy begins by understanding its definition, around which there is still much confusion. One can hear that confusion in the voices of HR Directors and Hiring Managers alike. This confusion can be quite costly. Every Agency seems to define Digital Strategy differently, and there are as many digital strategy jobs titles as there are Agencies.

We can think of Digital as the opposite of Analog. Anything not analog, or anything Smart (Smart Watch, Smart Phone, Smart Shoes) would be included under Digital Strategy. Think of your Apple Watch versus an analog watch, an electric guitar versus an acoustic guitar. Digital refers to something using discrete, often binary digits. Digital Technologies are electronic tools, systems, devices and resources that generate, store or process data. Well known examples include social media, online games, multimedia and mobile phones. Digital Strategy is formally defined as the use of technology to improve business performance by creating new products or reimagining current processes. It specifies the direction an organization will take to create new competitive advantages with technology, as well as the tactics it will use to achieve those changes. Digital Brand Design involves anything having to do with a brand's identity, community, conversation, category, or connections, i.e., things that are shareable, linkable, measurable, mobile, playable, programmable, or virtual. Social Media Strategy,

Mobile Strategy, Search Strategy (SEO) and E-commerce Strategy are elements of Digital Strategy. Bitcoin and Cryptocurrencies are quickly becoming a part of Digital Strategy as well. In the world of Advertising, Strategy and Digital Strategy fall under the Planning Department, which was introduced by British Advertising Agencies in the '60s and '70s to complement the work of the Creative Department. Planning and Strategy have a rich and storied past, and have become art forms in their own right. Advertising Agencies themselves can be broken into traditional Ad Agencies, Agency Networks, Creative Agencies, Media Agencies, and Digital or Social Agencies. The term Integrated Strategy refers to the collection of strategie disciplines across the entire Creative Agency, including, but not limited to: Planning, Creative Strategy, Production, Media Buying, Creative Technology, and Cross-Platform Strategy. Many Digital Strategists also think of themselves as Creative Strategists or Cultural Strategists given their proximity to creative campaigns and global culture. Some are also highly experienced Creative Technologists given their proximity to the product development process. Whichever direction you take (or hat you decide to wear), it's important to know the history and fundamentals of the profession so that you can move forward with confidence and clarity.

3

The Big Idea

So you've just finished watching a season or two of *Mad Men* or *Emily In Paris*. You're a budding influencer and avid Brand Ambassador. You love throwing parties, planning events, and shopping online. You have some design skills and your own online business. Your friends and family all turn to you for guidance when it comes to all things Social or Digital. You feel confident in your ability to guide them in the right direction, but have no formal training. Now you're ready to take things to the next level, but where do you start? If any of this sounds familiar then the next several chapters are for you.

Everyone approaches the business of Digital Strategy differently. Even seasoned professionals panic and stress at the start of a new piece of business or campaign. If you're Don Draper, you obsess for days and weeks, lash out at friends, family and colleagues, drink endlessly, and take long naps in the middle of the day. Hey, I'm not judging. But there is a better way. A more reliable and repeatable process. A more enlightened path. The Tao of Digital Strategy does exist and I'm here to guide you through it. Before you start to stress, sit back and relax, take a deep breath, and think about the big picture. What's the Big Idea you see running through your mind? What's the first thing that pops into your head? It doesn't have to be fully fleshed out or even make any sense just yet. It could be a color, a sound, a character, a concept, anything really. Whatever it is, write it down in as few sentences as possible. Record it on your phone, sketch it in your notebook, or find a link to it online. YouTube videos, previous campaigns, random stumbles, and good music are fantastic for this part of the process. The idea here is just to get the key elements of your idea on paper. This is the kernel of the idea. Now the real fun can begin. Strategy is 90% thinking and 10% doing. So think, what is it that excites you the most about the idea? What makes it worthwhile? Is it funny? Is it sad? Is it stupid, or is it silly? Believe it or not, random dumb ideas are often the way to go. Whatever it is that you love about it, write that down too. That's your Primer: Your key, your connector, your caption. Next, think about how this initial idea connects back to the brand, the client, or the business. What's true about the brand, the business, or the world that makes the idea funny, interesting or worthwhile? Write this down under the Primer and then take a short break. Now you've got your Kernel, your Primer, and your Truth. Grab a cup of coffee, walk around, stretch, reward yourself in some way. You've just started the Strategy Process and are looking much better than Don Draper. Now come back to the idea. Does it still ring true? Is it still funny or relevant or has it lost its original effect? If so, it's probably an idea worth pursuing and you should try to develop it further. If not, you haven't wasted much time and should feel free to move on to the next Big Idea. In Advertising we call this Ideation. It's the first step in the right direction. You can do it in groups or on your own, at the office, in the subway, or at the bar. The important thing is there's no wrong answer and no barrier to entry. Strategy is and always should be innately imaginative, playful and fun. Anyone can be strategic and creative. A good idea can come from anyone, anywhere, at any time. The key is to be open to ideas, inspiration and experimentation, not blocked off, bossy or afraid. Fear, angst, and anxiety are the enemy. Fun, friends, and humor are the good stuff. Once you've landed on a Big Idea that works, you're ready to start building your Digital Strategy. But first, let's take a look at where some of the best Big Ideas come from: Patterns, Trends, and Culture!

4

The Creative Process

Patterns, Trends, and Culture are probably the most exciting elements of Strategy. Go ahead, get excited! There aren't many professions where you get to be a part of global culture as opposed to a passive observer. Contrary to popular belief, Strategy is not some stale, stuffy process. Nor is it some stupid meme or momentary craze. Sure, memetics is a part of it, but it's not what Digital Strategy is all about. It's true that Strategy is a time-honored tradition, but it has more to do with the future than it has to do with the past. It is tied up with the present and connected to culture in a way that is dynamic, sexy and sophisticated. Patterns, Trends, and Culture can go unnoticed to the untrained eye. But to the Digital Strategist, they are the juicy elements all around us that can make a good idea great, and a great idea legendary! Budweiser's "Wassup" campaign, Bud Light's "Dilly Dilly!" "Got Milk?" "Beef, it's what's for dinner!" Nike's "Just Do It!" Gatorade's "Win From Within," and Sam Adams' "It's your cousin...from Boston!"

These aren't just some of the most memorable ads in our lives, they're some of the most memorable moments in our lives! Moments that change our moods and our minds, our economies, and the course of history itself. There is a connection between taglines and traditions, jingles and jams, slogans and language, language and literature, literature and meaning, meaning and purpose, purpose and significance, significance and existence, existence and truth, truth and time itself. All of these things are wrapped up in patterns, trends, and culture in ways that only the Digital Strategist knows how to decipher. That is the magic, the magnificence, the power and prestige of Digital Strategy. It is the reason that many of us go to "work" everyday and leave the office with smiles on our faces. It's what keeps us coming back to this business and never getting bored. It matters more than a paycheck, a fancy title, a new office, or honors, accolades and awards. It is a true calling, an unforgettable adventure, an awe inspiring opportunity, and a genuine art. AS any of the greats will tell you it's unlike any other industry in the world! Welcome!

5

The Brief

Alright, we've geeked out on culture. You've jotted down an idea of two. You've celebrated, had a drink and sat back and relaxed a bit. Now what? You could attack the brief, begin to uncover your brand barriers and tasks or start your research and positioning. You could also begin outlining your campaign architecture, mapping your campaign ecosystem or planning your campaign rollout. Lastly, you could develop your key performance indicators (KPIs), outline your analytics and reporting, or take some time to meet with your team or client. Every Strategist has their own process. Every Agency has their own preferences. The key is to stay flexible, inspired, and as creative as possible. For the purposes of our adventure, the process we just outlined will do. Before you begin your formal notes and research, it's usually a good idea to review the Client Brief, prepare a Creative Brief, and begin making informal notes on Communication Barriers and tactics. The client brief is just a fancy term for the information the client has provided about the brand, the business, and the requirements of the assignment or campaign. It typically includes information about the timing of the campaign, where it needs to appear, the budget, what the client is looking for, why the assignment is important, and any other considerations that should be included in the final delivery. In short, it tells you about the assignment and what needs to be delivered. The Creative Brief on the other hand is what you prepare for the Creative Team based on your reading and interpretation of the client brief. It outlines the tasks before the team, the requirements of the job, and other relevant information. It can be very long and detailed, or very short and sweet. It's your opportunity as the Digital Strategist to kick off the Creative Assignment and get the creative juices flowing. A good Creative Brief should open the door to creative possibilities rather than close them, and provide a solid foundation for the road ahead, much like surveyors preparing the field for Urban Planners. Be sure to make a note of any possible pitfalls or shortcomings in the client brief so you're prepared down the line. If there are any pieces of information missing or important questions remaining it's a good idea to talk to the Account team and get answers before it's too late. Advertising can be very political as various departments begin jockeying for position on certain accounts, like in the movie *What Women Want*. Watch out for the blame game and try to avoid having too many cooks in the kitchen. Communicate your needs and questions early. It's not your job to babysit the Creative team. Your job is to develop the best possible strategy for your client and inspire the best possible work from your Agency. If you feel politics are becoming an issue, talk to your boss about providing you some cover, and think about ways to start building a relationship with the client directly.

6

Research & Positioning

After the potential doldrums of the brief, comes another fun and exciting part of the Digital Strategy process: Research, Social Listening, and Positioning. This is my favorite part of the process because it requires the skills and mind of a true strategist. There are many different kinds of research that a strategist can perform: Formal and informal, qualitative and quantitative, primary and secondary, traditional and non-traditional. Every campaign is different with different requirements and approaches to research.

Different brands, different requirements. However, traditionally speaking, Strategists and Digital Strategists are usually expected (and should have) some kind of training or experience with formal Ethnography, Anthropology, Data Science and Analytics. This is because it's their job to understand and unpack the social, historical and psychological aspects of the brand, consumers, and the marketplace both individually and as a whole. Otherwise you're really not much use to anyone. Ethnography is the scientific description of the customs of individual peoples and cultures. Anthropology is the scientific study of humanity, concerned with human behavior, human biology, cultures and societies, in both the present and past, including past human species. Digital Anthropology is the anthropological study of the relationship between humans and digital-era technology. As mentioned, there are many forms this research can take. A good Strategist does both types of research simultaneously keeping one foot firmly planted in formal, quantitative, primary research and the other in informal, qualitative, secondary research so as to bring about a balance and abundance of ideas, information, and inspiration. This is where the Art and Science of Strategy come together, where patterns, trends and culture come to play a significant part. For some, this part of the process can seem a bit daunting, given the size of the Digital landscape and the diversity of research tools, platforms, and methodologies available. For others, this is the fun part where the real magic happens. Depending on the size of your team, it can be a good idea to divide and conquer. We all have different strengths and weaknesses and struggle or excel at different parts of the process. It's important to know what these are before the job begins, and to be supportive of everyone throughout the process, especially as managers or Senior Strategists. There can be a great deal of trial and error at this point, especially for recent graduates or Junior Strategists. Academic research can be very different from formal planning, so there has to be some room for training, knowledge sharing, and professional development. By the time you become a Group Strategy Director or VP of Strategy, you will have mastered every aspect of this process. You will be called upon to apply this knowledge and expertise to the effective management of your current clients, New Business pitches, and Executive Workshops. This is where legendary Strategists are made and Titanium Lions are won.

Next comes Social Listening, a critical (and widely misunderstood) part of the research process. Social Listening is the use of Social Media and Community Management tools to understand brand or category culture, conversation, and sentiment. It starts with a social audit and should include getting out into the real world to study your customers and consumers in the wild. Social Listening, as it's called, is a fairly new practice. It can involve rather advanced analytics tools, natural language processing platforms (NLPs), new Data Science techniques, media monitoring tools and more. The list of tools grows every year. Some of my favorite original players include Digimind, Hootsuite, Quid, and

Google Analytics. With the rise of AI and Machine Learning the types of tools available and their level of sophistication is evolving rapidly. An increasing number of the tasks originally performed by Social and Digital Strategists are now being performed by marketing and analytics automation tools like Lavalytics, Lexio and Thoughtspot. There have been 4 or 5 generations or waves of technologies, tools, and platforms over the years. I've seen, tested, and evaluated them all and even built and designed a few custom ones of my own. As great as the technology can get, it's important to remember that the tools we use are only as good as the Strategists who use them and the customers they support. Once you've completed your research and social listening it's time to start positioning the brand in the marketplace based on the insights you've collected. Let's go!

7

The Karate Belt System of Strategy

By now you're beginning to see just how much is involved in Digital Strategy. It's a tough but rewarding field. I know how you feel, but have no fear. Remember, the most important aspect of being an effective and successful Strategist is keeping a positive, playful, and creative attitude, and not letting fear or uncertainty get in the way. There can be stages to one's development as a Strategist; to help keep track of those stages and monitor your development, I've created the Karate Belt System of Strategy™. From White

Belts (Students and Beginners) to Black Belts (Group Strategy Directors and above) the game of Strategy is never over. Then there are Strategy Ninjas (Innovators & Impact). The Karate Belt System of Strategy is a great way to keep track of your progress. Never stop training:

Karate Belt System of Strategy™

White Belts
- Students & Beginners
- Strategy 101
- Patterns, Trends & Culture

Yellow Belts
- Social Strategists
- Community Management
- Communication & Branding Strategy

Green Belts
- Junior Strategists
- Data & Analytics
- Campaign Development

Blue Belts
- Senior Strategists
- Advanced Analytics & Reporting
- Campaign Architecture & Execution

Red Belts
- Group Strategy Director
- Portfolio Management
- Creative Technology

Brown Belts
- VP/SVP/EVP
- Executive Management
- Global Thought Leadership

Black Belts
- Chief Strategy Officers
- 360 Integrated Strategy
- Original Brand & Content Development

Ninjas
- Lions Winners & Jury Members
- Lecturers & Founders
- Innovators & Impact Experts

The next step in the Strategy process is Campaign Architecture. As any seasoned strategist will tell you, white boards and wall space are some of the most important utilities in a Strategist's toolbox. We like to put stuff up on walls. It's more important to the process than any technology or toolkit, especially at the early stages of brainstorming and ideation. With every new insight generated, a new piece of paper, flashcard or post-it note is added to the board. This way everyone can keep track of the process and any updates as they come. Since slide decks, power-points and "pitch decks" are the main deliverables of the Strategy process, pin-boards are the perfect way to see the campaign evolve and unfold. You can think of it as a moving storyboard with elements of a Gantt Chart, proposal, prospectus, and timeline. It outlines the entire strategy from research and positioning to execution. It's typically broken into sections that match the structure of the strategy itself: Identity, Community, Conversation, Category, and Consumer. Another way to think of this is as a Strategy Bible or Playbook composed of the individual pieces of the overall strategy. It is, essentially, your recommendation to the Brand or Client. Sometimes it's broken into pieces and presented to internal and external audiences in different ways. This modular approach to Strategic Development is the very foundation and essence of effective Strategy. It can make or break the development of an idea, and certainly impacts the quality of client pitches and New Business opportunities. Those who master it are the Strategists that go on to win awards, lead great teams, and become Strategy Ninjas. When done right, modular ideation can make campaign architecture a breeze. This is because by the time you complete the process, your architecture is already in place. Then it's just a matter of arranging your oral arguments for your various audiences. This way you move from strategic order to creative order and campaign order seamlessly and effortlessly.

So what does a good campaign structure look like? First and foremost, everything ladders up and connects to create a seamless flow of ideas and outcomes. The form of things compliments their function and how the tactics roll-out over the course of the campaign. There is no fluff or excess. No disconnects or drop offs. There is nothing arbitrary or superfluous about the strategy or architecture unless done so purposefully. This, my friend, is Strategy. Not some idle meme or hashtag, not some tagline, mascot or jingle alone. This is the difference between good brands and great brands, good work and great work, awesome ideas and legendary Agencies. Synergy is key. Substance, Science and Art come together to transform a category or market, even a country.

Just watch the movie *No!* (Participant Media) to see what's possible as a Strategic and Creative leader in this business.

8

Campaign Ecosystem & Rollout

Once you've organized your campaign architecture, it's time to add your campaign ecosystem and rollout. Each of these is typically a single page or two; they can also appear as a large diagram or consumer journey. Wherever and however they appear, it's important that they're clear, precise, and well organized. Sure, these documents can and do change and evolve, but it's important that they remain consistent and accurate as they do. Clients expect to follow along and see these documents in action; if there are too many changes and inconsistencies, they can begin to lose confidence and trust in your strategy. The same goes for Creative Teams and Agency Leadership. Precision, timing, and consistency are the responsibility of Strategy and should be done right the first time. This is the essence of a good Strategy.

You can think of an Ecosystem as a list of all the channels, places, and platforms across which the campaign will appear, as well as all the ways in which it will be seen: Print, TV, Radio, Out of Home (OOH), Digital, Social, Events, etc. Wherever you plan to show up in the world, be sure to include it in your Ecosystem. It's also important to include any branded assets and channels (owned or operated by the Brand) you plan to utilize. A Campaign Rollout illustrates the timing and sequence of these items as they relate to the launch or lifespan of the campaign. Together, they are the 5Ws of your Strategy and should align with the audiences you intend to reach. These documents appear in many forms and places, shapes and sizes. The important thing is that they're clear, logical and complete. As a Client or

Executive seeing everything for the first time, I want to be able to take one look at these documents and understand the campaign. I also want to be able to follow along as things unfold and chart our progress as we go. The order of things is just as important as the big picture itself. I should be able to follow your thinking, understand the critical element and individual pieces of the puzzle very quickly and easily. In short, they should be able to withstand pressure testing, questions, and the fast-moving world of Media and Entertainment. Like a good game of Battleship, no boat should go undefended or left on its own.

9

KPIs, Analytics & Reporting

Once your Campaign Architecture, Ecosystem and Rollout are clear and complete, it's time to finalize how you're going to measure and evaluate your campaign. What metrics will you use to measure your success and when and how will they be reported to the client? These are known collectively as your Key Performance Indicators (KPIs), Analytics, and Reporting Cadence. They will help you understand your campaign success and effectiveness, and share that knowledge with your team and client. This is a major part of your role as the keepers of all things Data and Analytics related. It is your power, and with great power comes great responsibility to maintain effectiveness, rigor and authenticity. Your KPIs should correspond with the Business Objectives and Goals you and your client established at the outset. When formulating your KPIs it's important to remember why the client or brand came to you in the first place. What were their business objectives? What did they hope to accomplish, and to what extent did you meet those expectations? Given the nature of Digital Media, it's also important to know how you plan to continue measuring those things, and how your campaign compares to everything else on the market. Your objectives, KPIs, and analytics should be clear, precise and consistent with what you're trying to measure and report. They can be both qualitative and quantitative, forward-facing and backward-looking. A good rule to follow here is KISS: Keep It Simple Stupid. Clients are not Mathematicians or Data Scientists. That's what they expect you to be. Don't waste their time with complex formulas and statistics. Just show them what you plan to measure, how you plan to measure it, and what it all means for their brand. These metrics typically fall into five buckets and are measured and reported using an extensive list of tools, platforms, and technologies. Tangible metrics like Brand Lift, Share of Voice, Sentiment, and overall ROI are important here. Now kick back and celebrate…you're done!

10

Putting It All Together

Congratulations, you've made it! You're now ready to move forward with your careers and campaigns with confidence. You should feel good. You know what you're doing now and can demonstrate your skills formally and professionally. This is just the beginning! Enjoy the feeling. A lifetime of strategic leadership, excellence, and awards await! Strategists are not born, they're made. It's a trial by fire, through endless pitch decks and presentations, big ideas and bad executions. If you're lucky you'll meet a few powerful

Brands and brave Creatives along the way. Remember, Creatives may get the limelight, but Strategists are the real deal, the substance and creative spark of the industry; they are the connection between the first word of the brief and the final TV commercial. We don't just breathe life into original ideas, we shepherd them in and out of the world, and we do so without ego, excuses, or enmity. We practice what we preach and let our talent do the talking. Our purpose is proven out time and time again. We instill confidence in our teammates and bring clarity and criticality to everything we do. Our job is not to complicate or convolute, but to elevate and expand. We seek to simplify and signify, adding significance and impact at every stage. Minimalism, meaning, motion and emotion are our gifts, and we apply our craft wisely. Strategy represents the best of the creative process. It may not seem like it to some, but it is actually the cool part, the originality and authenticity of the creative delivery. What's more, it is the foundation and wellspring of intellectual property, the very thing of value and economy itself.

Consumers may purchase a product or service, but what they're really buying is a brand. And behind every brand are somewhat seamless elements of strategy. A Strategist's education is never over, it never ends. We are constant students and observers of culture—Ethnographers, Anthropologists, Psychologists and Sociologists. We bring a sense of history, philosophy, literature and logic to the sometimes shallow world of advertising, brands and business. As Digital Strategists, we transform traditional brands and industries into modern and meaningful businesses. We give them significance and reach beyond just a logo, product line or brick and mortar presence. If Digital Transformation and Product Innovation are indeed the only two ways to grow a business, then the significance of the Digital Strategist is truly great. Our job is never done. Digital Transformation is an evergreen process and an $11 trillion industry. It will be you, dear reader, the Digital Strategists of the future who get to claim the largest portions of that prize. Earn your belts with honor and dignity as every student of martial arts must. From one Strategist to another I say, go forth and create!

ABOUT THE AUTHOR

Champion Muthle aka Daniel Maree is an award-winning Writer-Director, Creative and Cultural Strategist. He has worked in Strategy for The World Bank, McCann, Havas, TBWA, and a number of other companies, including his own Digital Strategy Consultancy. He has received over a dozen Advertising Awards including 2 Cannes Lions, 2 Clios, 2 Art Director Awards, a Webby and a D&AD Silver Pencil nomination. He is a Frederick Douglass Scholar and Forbes 30 Under 30 Honoree for Social Entrepreneurship. His work has been featured in the MoMA and the Library of Congress.